I0494537

Stass Paraskos

edited by Michael Paraskos
with essays by John Cornall,
David Haste, Norbert Lynton
and Benedict Read

The **Orage** Press

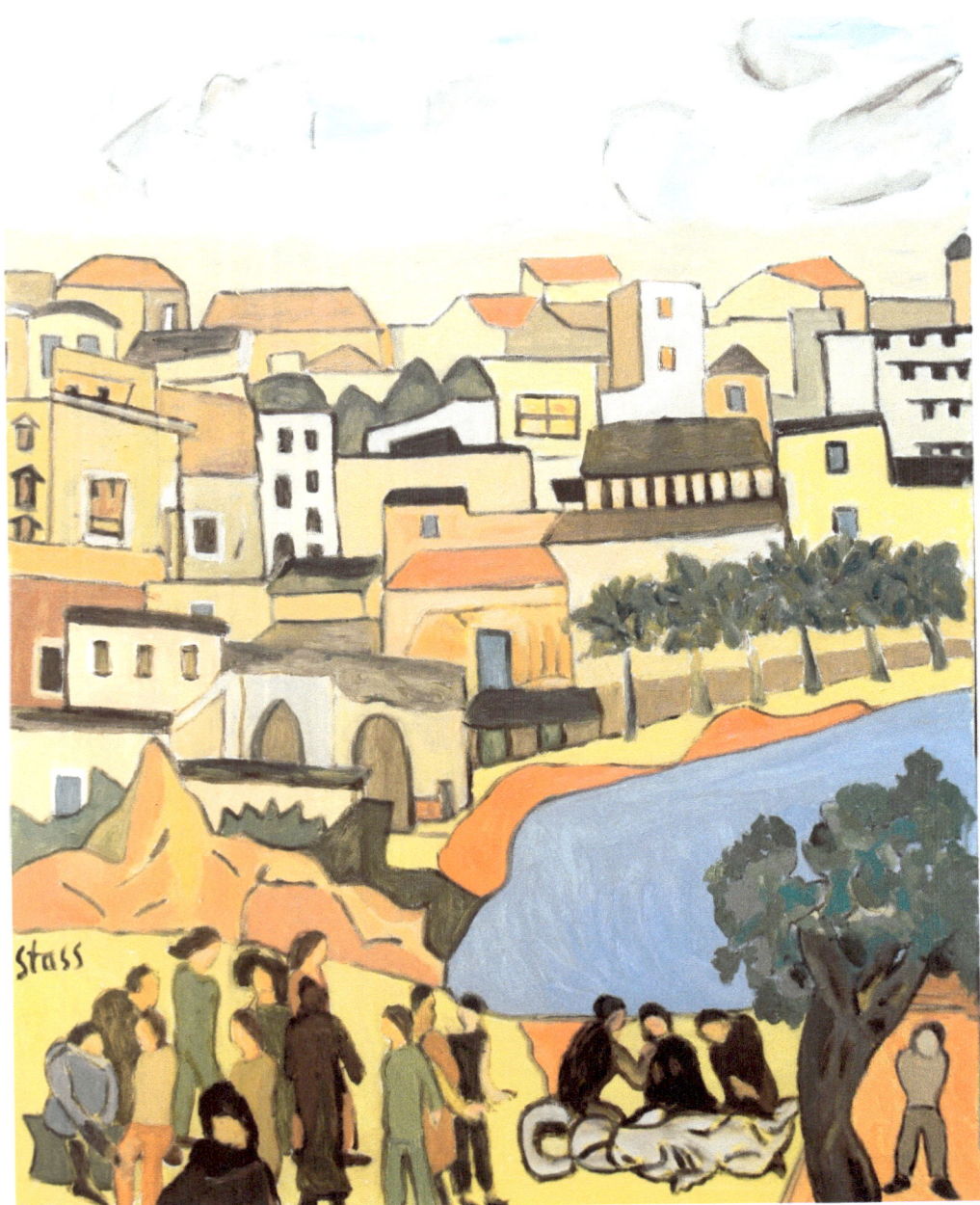

St Lazaros of Larnaca, oil on canvas, 2008

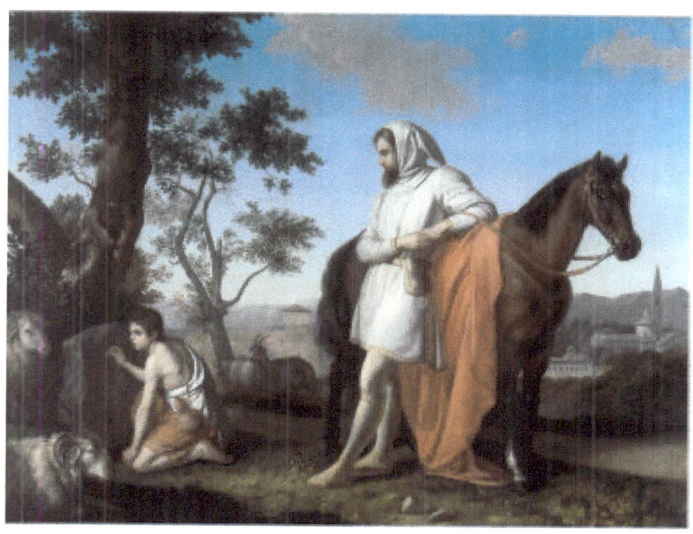
Cimabue Finding Giotto by Gaetano Sabatelli

The Italian Renaissance artist and art-historian, Giogio Vasari, begins his life of the artist Giotto (1266-1337) with the declaration: 'the debt owed by painters to Nature ... serves them continually as an example, that from her they may select the best and finest parts for reproduction and imitation.' The pioneering exemplar of this, according to Vasari, was Giotto who had a supreme impact on the development of Renaissance art. Vasari explains how this came about. Aged 10, Giotto was set by his father to serve as shepherd; while following the sheep from place to place to find pasture, Giotto 'was always drawing something from Nature or representing the fancies which came into his head, on flat stones on the ground or on sand, so much was he attracted to the art of design by his natural inclination'.

In this situation, the young Giotto was spotted by the eminent senior painter Cimabue. Cimabue 'came upon Giotto, who, while his sheep were grazing, was drawing one of them from life with a roughly pointed piece of stone upon a smooth surface of rock, *although*

STASS
PARASKOS

Benedict Read

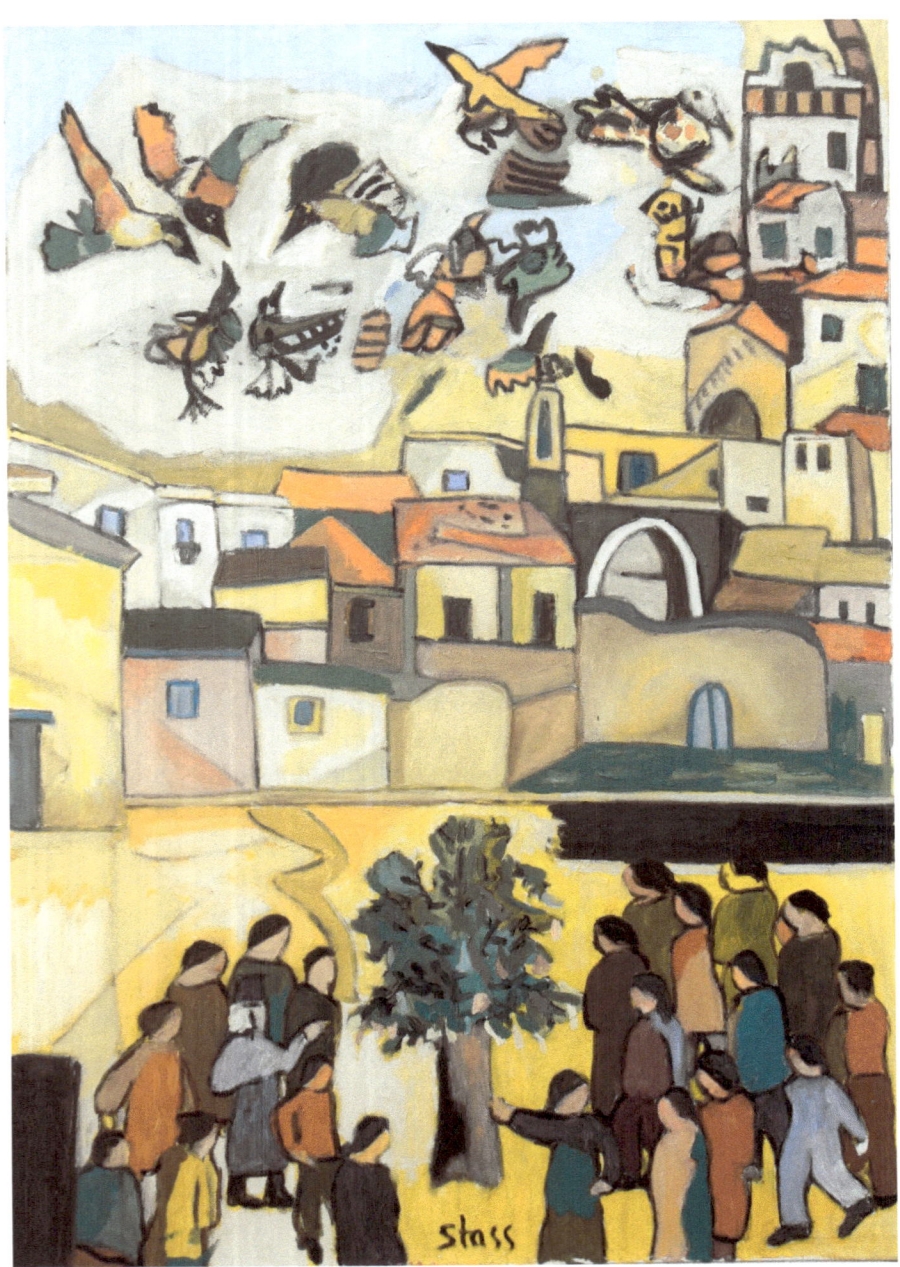

Birds Above the Village, oil on canvas, 2008

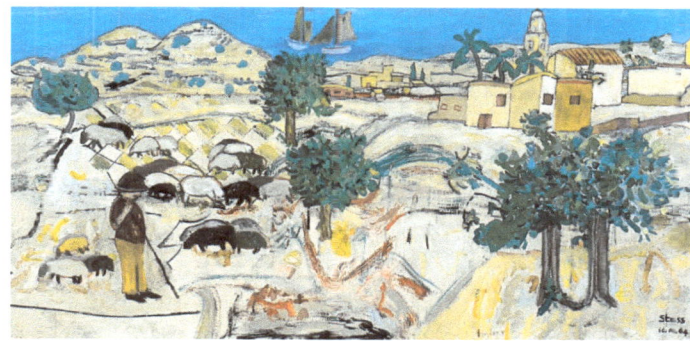

The Shepherd, oil on board, 1964

he had never had any master but Nature' [my italics].
Cimabue was so impressed, he took the boy into his own
studio and from there he developed into one of the major
pioneers of Italian painting.

Stass Paraskos grew up in rural Cyprus and as a
boy he tended his uncle's sheep near the village of
Anaphotia. While he was not discovered there drawing
from nature - his Cimabue moment was to come later -
there can be no doubt that his direct experience of nature
started in such circumstances and one can walk with
Stass today and hear him respond to the myriad forms
and colours of plants, stones and soil, whether in the
countryside that still survives beyond the concrete jungle
that has taken over much of Cyprus, or in the built-up
areas where gardens bloom everywhere and waste land
can display an array of plants; even the urban dual
carriageways are lined with highly-coloured flowering
shrubs. As I shall explain further, the colours of Cypriot
nature are fundamental to Stass's work.

The Cimabue in Stass's life was the great
revolutionary art teacher in Leeds in the 1950s and 60s,
Harry Thubron. As a young man Stass came to England
and enrolled at Leeds College of Art. He was soon
spotted by Thubron, then Head of Painting, who more or
less ordered his academic colleagues to leave Stass well
alone, as there was already such a unique artistic

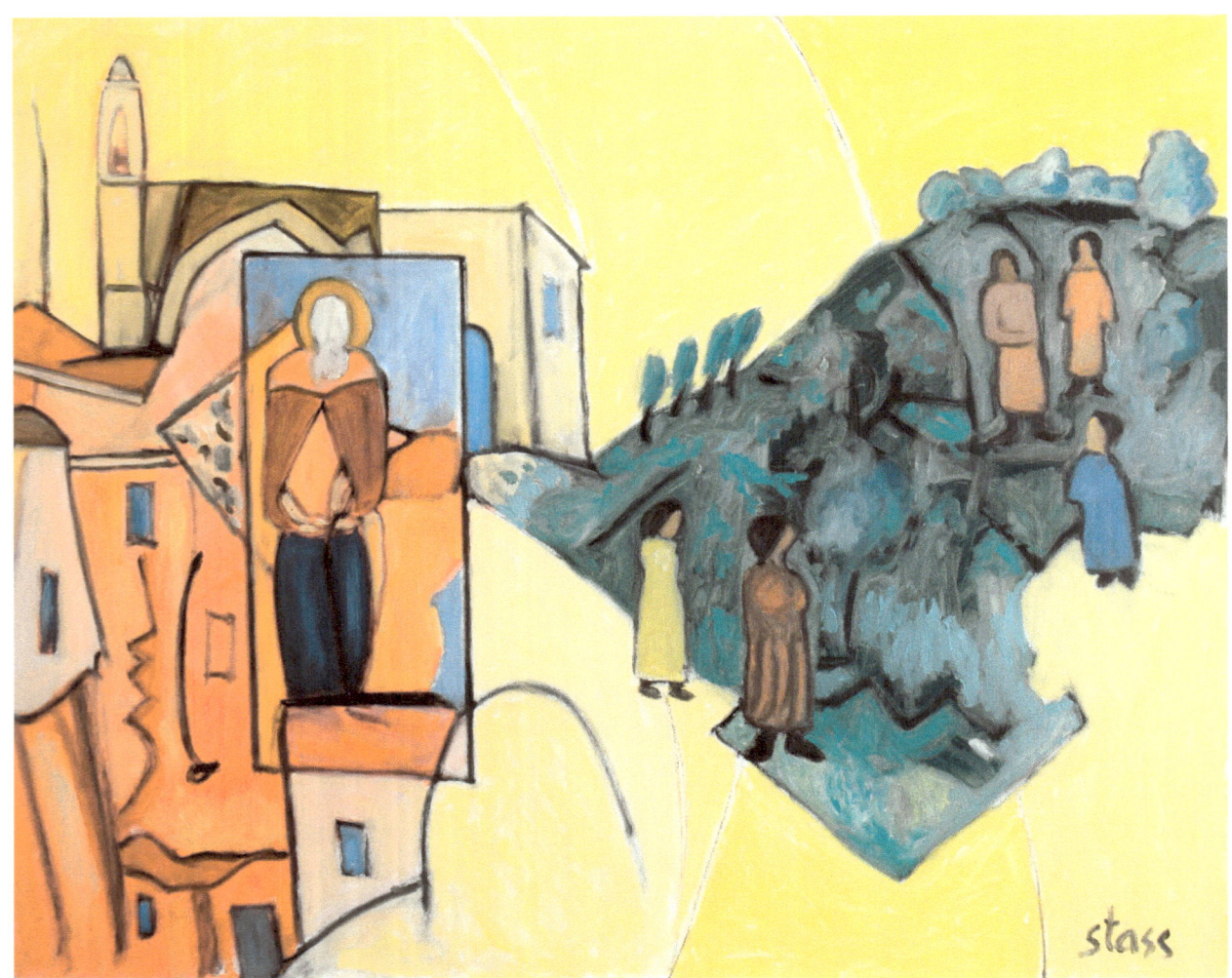

Saint with Women in the Fields, oil on canvas, 2008

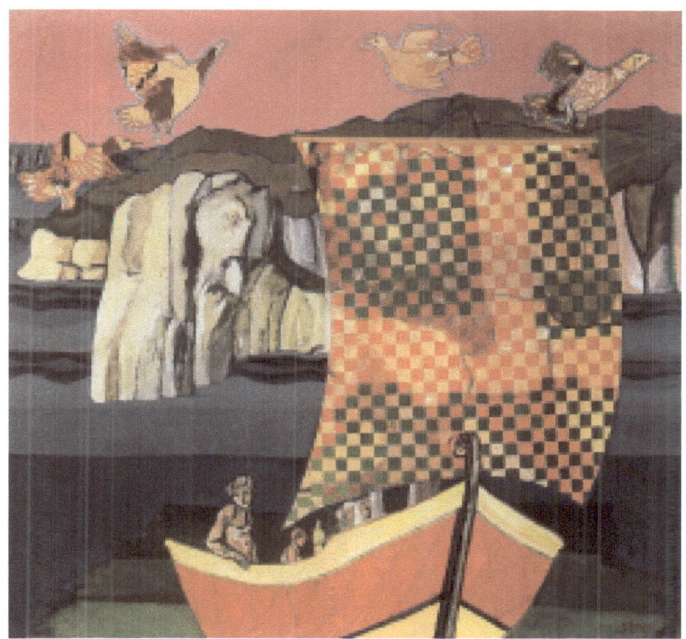

Liberty Abandons Cyprus, oil on canvas, 1972

personality there and he should not be interfered with by humdrum academic formulas. Of course, Stass still learnt then and later about a range of techniques for art making. Similarly there is no doubt Stass learned something from other artists and he is continually looking at what others have made or are making. He openly acknowledges his respect for Ben Nicholson - see his *Homage to Ben Nicholson* of 1962 - and talks about the importance of Van Gogh. Norbert Lynton sees the influence of Gauguin and Matisse, whilst John Cornall talks about the importance of ancient Levantine art from Egypt and Syria. But in a way these are not so much cases of 'influence', let alone imitation, it is more a matter of consanguinity, a sharing of ideas and values, which is the reason why Stass's interests can range so far and wide.

Overall, Stass's subject matter is Cyprus. There are many scenes of village life, going to church, having meetings, or simply people gathering. But they are not always quite as simple as they seem and can incorporate a layering of indigenous history, past and contemporary. Some may be memories of village life, with women going to church, men holding meetings or going to the coffee shop. Others can incorporate birds as symbols of freedom, reflecting the traumas of Cyprus's recent political history. One work of 1972, now in the State Gallery in Nicosia, is called *Liberty Abandons Cyprus,* and reflects the troubled times of recent Cyprus history. There are refugee scenes too, and another series of works features corpses derived from news images of the Israeli invasions of Lebanon, a country immediately adjacent to Cyprus. There are scenes incorporating people bathing, which might be drawn from the sight of the many thousands of holidaymakers Stass sees each summer visiting Cyprus, but at the same time they may draw on much older ideas, as seen in one image that seems to show the Three Graces on the beach. There are scenes of lovers in the community, but these sometimes represent at the same time the Adoration of Aphrodite, the ancient Greek Goddess of Love whom legend claims came ashore not far from Paphos.

Stass's figure scenes are often set in a townscape or landscape, but there is a symbolic ordering of figures. The landscape is based on nature, but it is not schematised in the way Western art has been since the Renaissance. It is much more a formalised sense of space, like what we see in certain of the amazing Byzantine narrative paintings that survive in Cyprus, such as the *Raising of Lazarus from the Dead* in the church of Ayia Paraskevi at Yeroskipou of the 15th century, or *The Nativity of Christ* from the main church at the Monastery of St. Neophytos near Paphos, dating from the beginning of the 16th century. Other examples can be found in the UNESCO-listed churches in the Troodos mountains. None of this should be a surprise granted the cultural significance of their Byzantine identity for the Greek inhabitants of the island and we find other scenes incorporating saints in Stass's depictions of life that are ambiguous in their time-setting. There may even be an additional, significant debt in Stass's work to the aesthetics of Byzantine art, in which the artwork is not just a representation of a place or scene, but more a gateway, or metaphysical portal, to an inner truth, and this maybe is how we can understand the apparent ambiguities to be found so often in Stass's work.

There can be no doubt that the colouring of Stass's paintings directly reflects the natural array of colours on the island of Cyprus. The rocks themselves range from cream to yellow to beige, the mountains can be blue, grey or purple, there is a range of shades of green at all times of year, while the colour of the sea can be wine-dark (as Homer described), grey, a range of blues, even silver - all dependent on the nature of the light in the changing atmosphere and season. Even today Stass inaugurates the teaching of his students at the Cyprus College of Art, where he is Principal, by telling them to go out and observe and record four colours that they can see in the landscape. By doing this, he suggests, they will produce work imbued with the spirit of the place. And this is the summary of his lifelong practice of art – go to Nature and the rest will follow. For Stass this has always been a fundamental part of the art of Cyprus, but as his many students over the years, whether taught by him at Leeds, Leicester, Canterbury, Cyprus or elsewhere, will testify, it is good advice and practise for an artist wherever they are.

Stass's paintings have developed over the years, in manner and in content, though their essential character, which is also his, remains constant. I nearly wrote 'and in ambition', but from the first he has produced 'simple' still lifes and figure subjects, as well as occasional paintings that tackle more polemical subjects, often on a larger scale. Stylistically, it seems to me, he moved quite rapidly from a relatively graphic idiom to one that is wholly painterly. I mean by this that in the earlier work, until the early 1970s, he was drawing lines with the brush and filling forms in as and where he needed them, but leaving the picture quite light, usually with a white or pale ground. From the mid-1970s on he has painted more full-bloodedly, producing pictures full of colour – sometimes also quite dark paintings (which are difficult to reproduce effectively) – and altogether developing a pictorial idiom that can communicate lyrically but, when required, also dramatically to deliver grave themes. Much of his art comments affectionately on humanity's ordinary ways in its everyday doings.

When Stass had his 1966 solo exhibition at the Leeds Institute, up a steep staircase, in a room occasionally used for exhibitions, one of his graphic paintings, entitled *Lovers and Romances,* and some drawings related to it, caused a great rumpus. They are small, undramatic images about love. In the bottom left-hand corner of the painting is a man and a woman, naked, more outlined than painted, without emphasis on the two bodies as physical objects. She is seated across his lap. We can make out two lines that may signal the first inch of the man's penis. They are kissing; there is no indication of further sexual action. These are light and lyrical pictures, romantic rather than sensual.

Two schoolgirls had been heard giggling. Someone alarmed the Leeds police. Technically speaking this was a public display, though very much inside the Institute and for the College of Art around the

THE TRIAL
Norbert Lynton

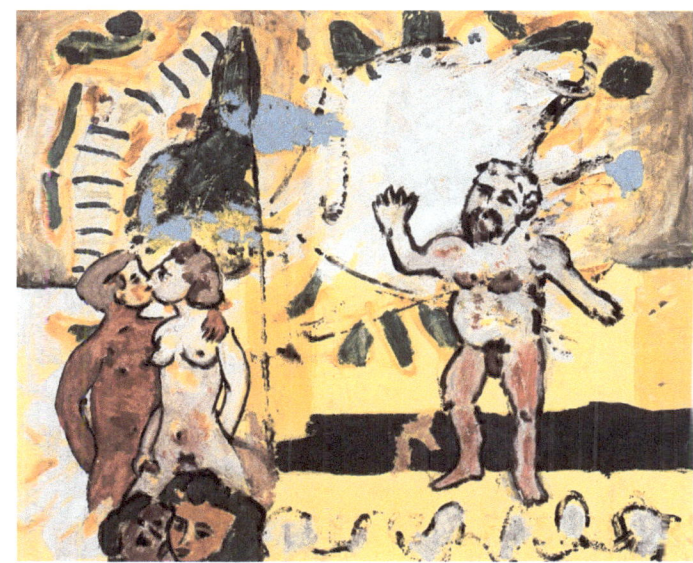

Lovers and Romances, oil on board, 1966

corner. The police seized the offending works, and Stass was accused, under Vagrancy Acts of 1824 and 1838 of 'publishing an obscenity'. (The question whether it was not the College that was actually guilty of 'publishing' this art was never asked. Easier to go for the individual.)

The trial must have been a painful experience for him: a strange situation in a strange country. Today we are all more relaxed about these things, and the accused might well be heroicized by the media. Even then, the press, reporting the trial, seemed surprised at the fuss: would this prosecution have happened in London? The trial took place before three magistrates. For two days, people called as 'expert witnesses' by the defence spoke up for the quality and inoffensiveness of the pictures: Sir Herbert Read, the world-famous poet, art critic and educationalist; Professor Quentin Bell of the Fine Art Department of Leeds University, artist and author as well as critic; John Jones, artist and film- maker, who worked with Quentin Bell; myself, by then head of art history at

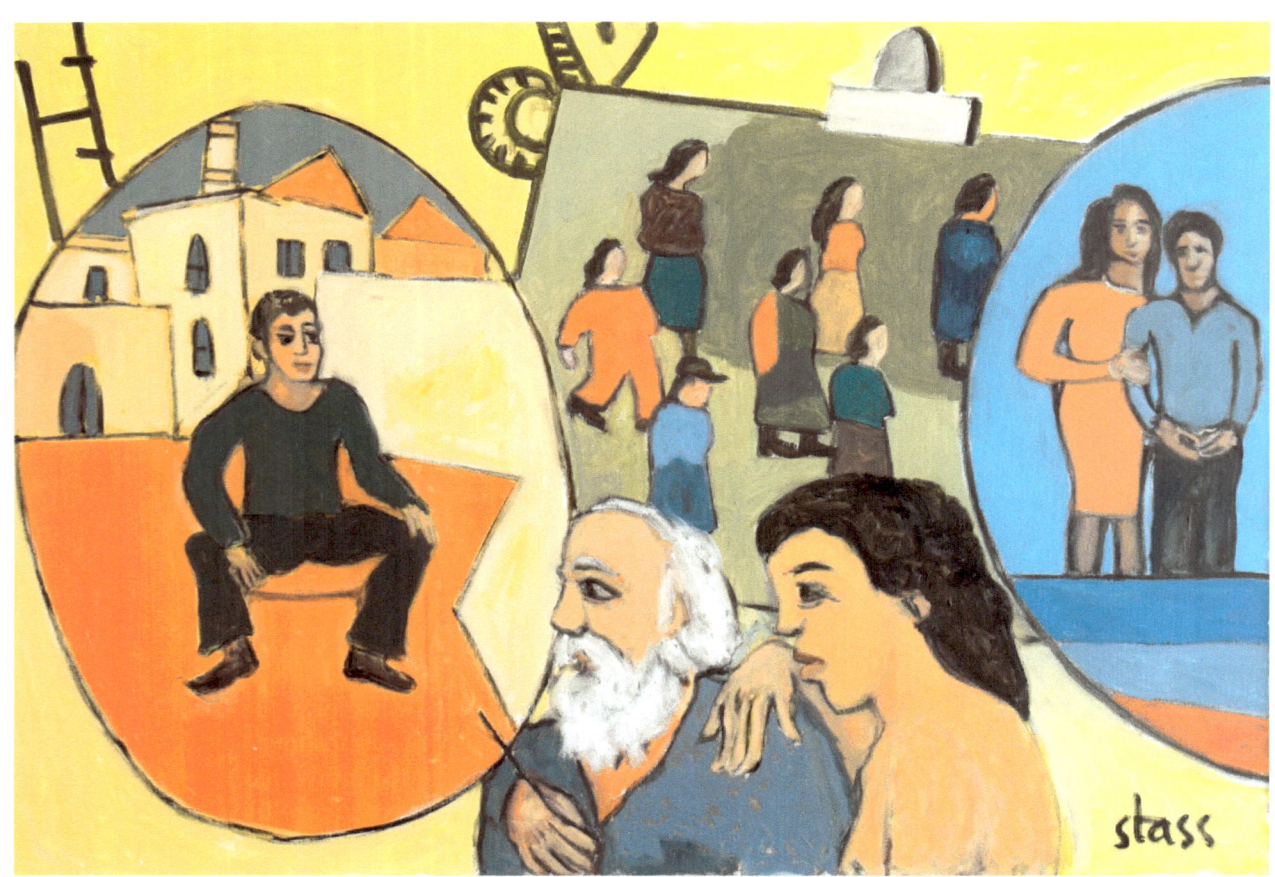

The Artist, oil on canvas, 2008

Chelsea School of Art in London and *The Guardian's* art critic. We did our best to sound reasonable. I recall being asked what I would think if I 'saw this kind of thing going on in the street outside', and tried to explain that poetry and art were not the same sort of reality as daily life – that, for instance, when we were hungry we might go to a café or a restaurant but certainly not into an art gallery to feast on a still life. What if we saw a man being crucified in the street? It was all a waste of time. 'Mr Paraskos' was found guilty. It was said the pictures would be destroyed, but in fact they were returned to him and a fine was imposed. Not too grave a matter? It lives on in Stass's mind.

The most immediate consequence was two-fold. The head of Leeds College of Art, Eric Taylor, arranged for Stass to be given part-time teaching: two days a week. Stass had already, since 1963, been teaching under Tom Hudson at the Leicester School of Art. To be teaching in, so to speak, his own College was an additional confirmation of respect, especially after that prosecution. The other consequence of the trial was that there was talk in London of raising the question of obscenity laws as relating to this instance in Parliament. No one thought them effective or satisfactory (they have been amended since, but the situation remains unsatisfactory, as it must in a such private-public matters where people generally want freedom for themselves but often seem to feel that others need the protection of censorship). Stass received letters from the Home Office, signed by the eminent politician Tom Driberg, who was writing on behalf of the even more eminent Roy Jenkins (the late Lord Jenkins, then Home Office Minister in Harold Wilson's government). They expressed sympathy for Stass; this would not happen again, and if Stass cared to let the Home Office know when he was next exhibiting work in London, the Minister would make a point of coming to see the work and bring with him

Jennie Lee, the admirable Labour Member of Parliament who was Minister for the Arts. Britain has a gift for fudging issues where morality and law conflict, but this unambiguous encouragement – implying, if not actually stating, disagreement with the court's decision – was both bold and admirable. And Stass was invited to show his work at London's prestigious Institute of Contemporary Arts (the ICA).

Terry Frost was the Gregory Fellow in Painting at Leeds University during 1954- 6 and got involved with the Leeds College of Art, teaching there for three years after the Fellowship ended. He encouraged Stass to spend some time in St Ives where Frost was a leading member of the so-called St Ives School of artists which included Ben Nicholson, Barbara Hepworth, Patrick Heron, Roger Hilton, Peter Lanyon and other notable individuals. Most of them were producing abstract art, or art much abstracted from visual reality, often in expressive idioms which reflected the space, colours and dynamics of the Cornish land and seascape. Just as Frost's work was affected by his experience of Yorkshire, so Stass's was enriched by what he found among the St Ives artists, but a major by-product of these visits to south-west England and that busy creative scene was that Stass could know himself as one of them, with his own character, priorities and ideals, but unquestionably part of an active, disputatious as well as often positively friendly, world of living artists. His work gained in strength. He had close on twenty solo exhibitions in the 1960s, and he was sought after as a teacher, even becoming Senior Lecturer in Painting at the Canterbury College of Art, later known as the University of Creative Arts.

As a last acolade flowing on from the trial, however, the drawings that caused the fuss in 1966 were finally acquired in 2006 by the same British state that had once prosecuted the artist for showing them, and they now reside in London's Tate Gallery.

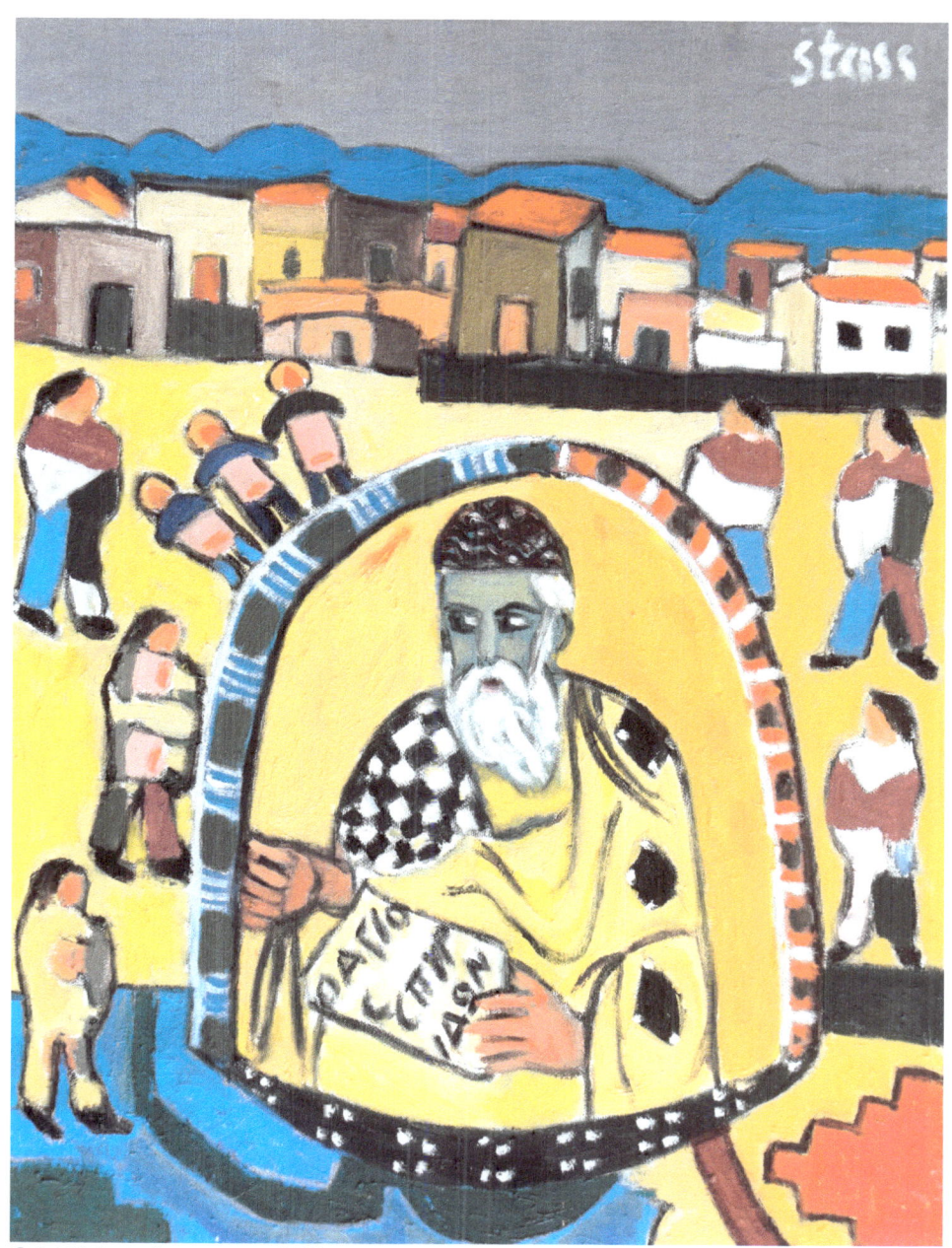

Saint (Ayios), oil on canvas, 2008

Paraskos's life story, his sensualism, his native directness and his cosmopolitanism, all suggest ways of interpreting his painting, especially the narrative paintings. But even when his art does bear a personal or autographic reference this always exists alongside a secondary public, and specifically Cypriot, meaning.

Take his painting *The Painter* for example. In it, the character of the painter sits comfortably in a room, bright and delicious, like a Matisse interior, whilst at the window, the old ladies from the village peer in, grimacing and snickering, earthily real. In another work, the painter appears again, this time naked and athletic looking. He has been caught by a priest whilst carrying off a fulsome nude (a nude on a canvas not a real woman). The priest eyes him sternly, Bible-wielding, posed like the Pantocrator.

If these are personal paintings then they are impersonally personal because the personal is representative of the whole. The painter character, for example, *could* be Paraskos, and on one level he is; but he could also represent one facet of the intrinsic character of Cypriotness. Paraskos poses a clash of cultures, or perhaps not a clash but a predicament, even a dialectic, that applies personally but which also applies to the island of Cyprus, to that strange co-mingling of sensualism and religion that is at the heart of all things in Cyprus: the sleepy servant of the Levant coiled around the hard rock of Byzantium.

Although Paraskos is ardently a Cypriot artist, he is not a Nationalist. He objects in plain terms to the way the politicians and Church in Cyprus play a nationalist ticket, distorting history for their own ends. These and other opinions Paraskos has dealt plainly in his shoot-from-the-hip popular poetry and in his writings for newspapers. He is the man who stands apart from the crowd, the *real* Cypriot, as *Enimerosi* once called him. It follows that when Paraskos's art invokes Cypriot styles and traditions it never does so simply or gratuitously, as a Nationalist art does. The Cypriotness is not a mere costume language or dress for

STASS AND CYPRIOTNESS
John Cornall

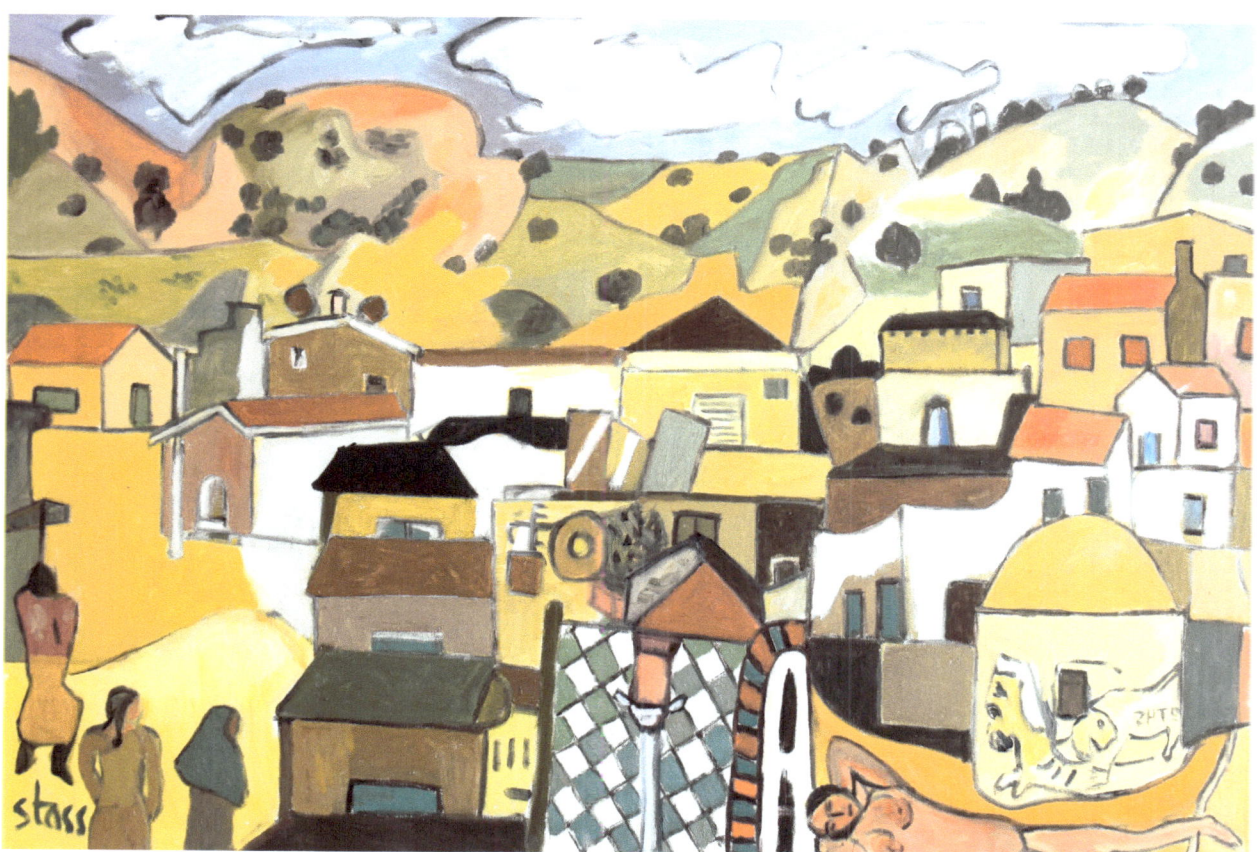

Village in the Landscape, oil on canvas, 2008

service. Paraskos's Cypriot art is traditional but it has, in the case of the narrative paintings, a discursive content, so simply, in the case of the decorative work, an edge that challenges. The result is that one cannot imagine his art, even in the future, being used in the way that Niko Pirosmanashvili's paintings are used by the Georgian government and tourist industry. This does not mean the Georgian 'Pirosmani' is less good a painter than Paraskos, nor does it mean that either painter does not in their own way express a national psyche in their arts – as the brochures might put it. What it does mean is that Paraskos is not an innocent primitive. Further to this, the dualism in the Cypriot character that Paraskos describes is not a *fait accomplie,* or fixed idea. Cypriotness is adumbrated in terms of a process or a dialectical struggle, if you like, through which Cyprus evolves. Paradoxically, Cyprus must free itself from its own ideas of 'self' to ensure the enrichment and continuity of its traditions, a fact which is made clear in the paintings Paraskos produced for the Sao Paolo Bienale in 1996.

Of course, it would be easy to misunderstand Paraskos's position with regard to Nationalism. One of Paraskos's favourite paintings, called *Folk Motif,* which he keeps in his home, is a painterly version of a popular poster he once found portraying, in a crude but bold symmetrical design, the photographed faces of heroes of EOKA fighters who fought against the British in Cyprus in the 1950s. Their leader George Grivas is shown in the middle. Paraskos liked the crudity and naivety of the poster, which reminded him of the posters that Zaffalis had made in the 1950s. So to Paraskos the crude nationalist poster had more artistic merit than what a more sophisticated version of the same poster might have had. It also betrayed the influence of genuine folk traditions, was iconic and had a strong unashamed sense of sentiment. These were the factors Paraskos sought to capture in his own painting, but when he tried to present the work to the Museum of the National Struggle in his

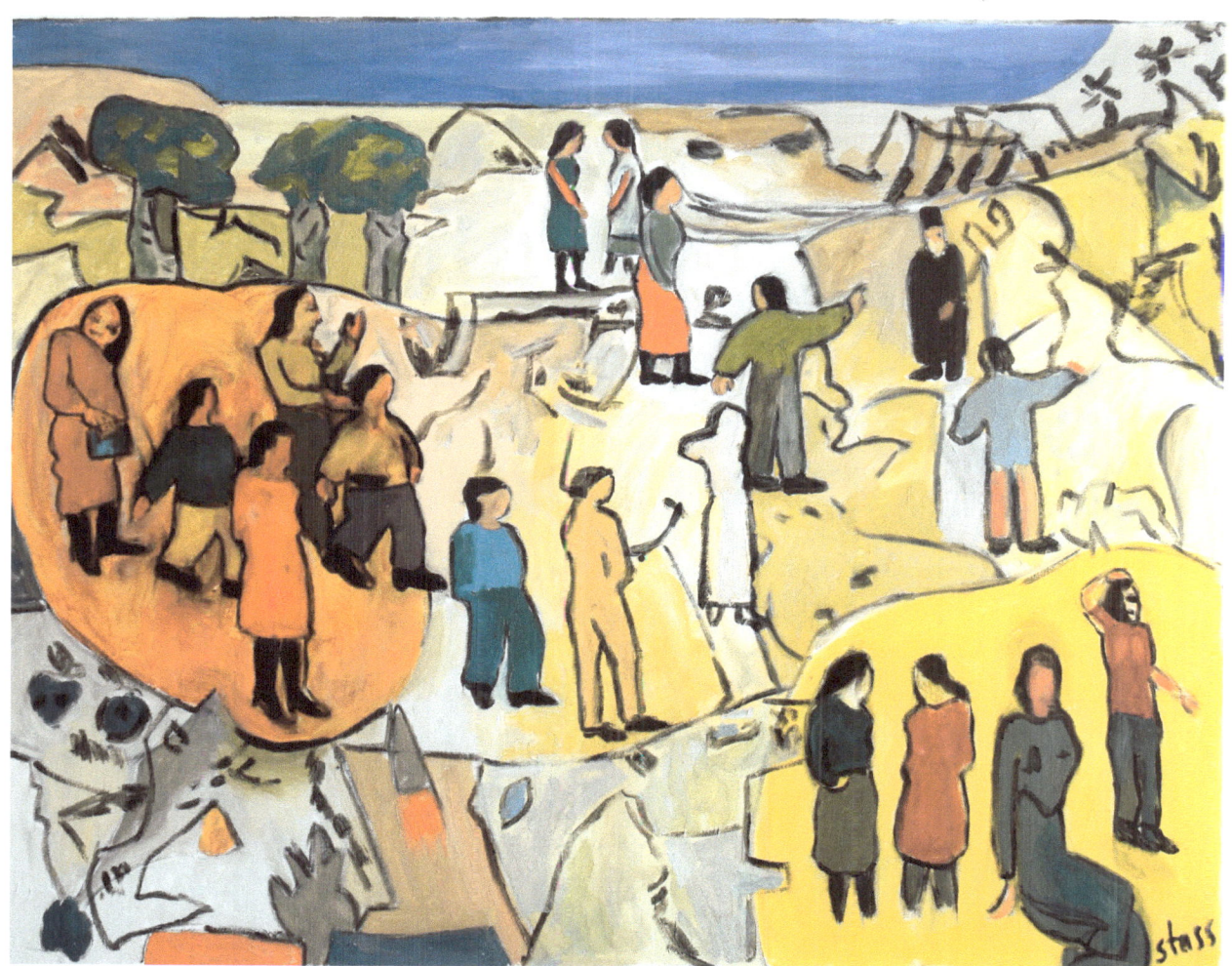

Sunday Morning, oil on canvas, 2008

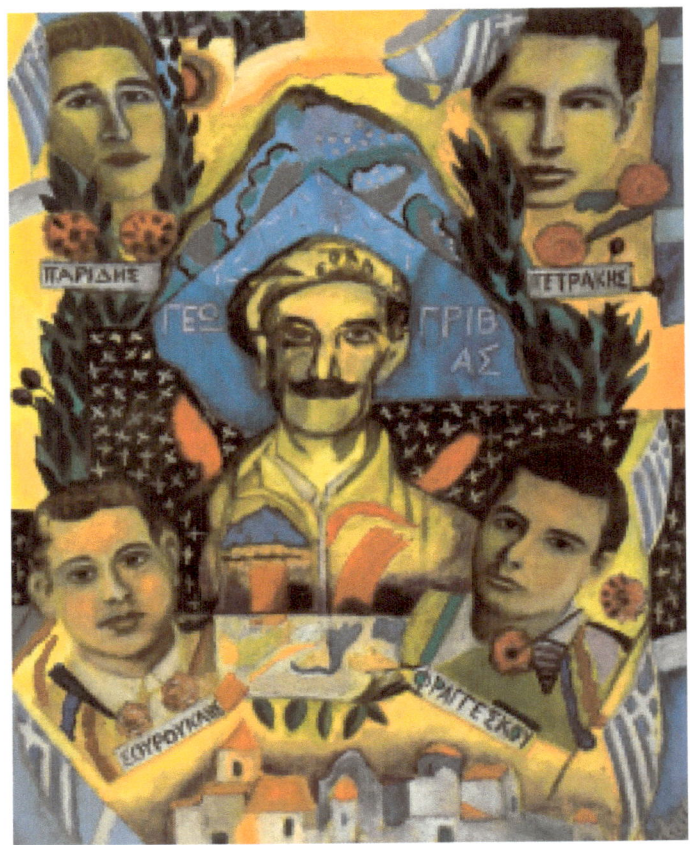

Folk Motif, oil on canvas, 1991

home town of Larnaca, it was rejected for being too crude. The museum's governors wanted an official celebration of the idea of Grivas as the martial *Dighenis,* the national hero, and could not see that Paraskos was paying an entirely different kind of homage – celebrating the loving spirit of the ordinary Cypriot.

Paraskos believes Cypriots have always had a natural eye for design, and that this found its purest expression in popular or folk art forms. From this he has made his own 'folk objects', including a set of decorative wooden reliefs, rather like the hanging

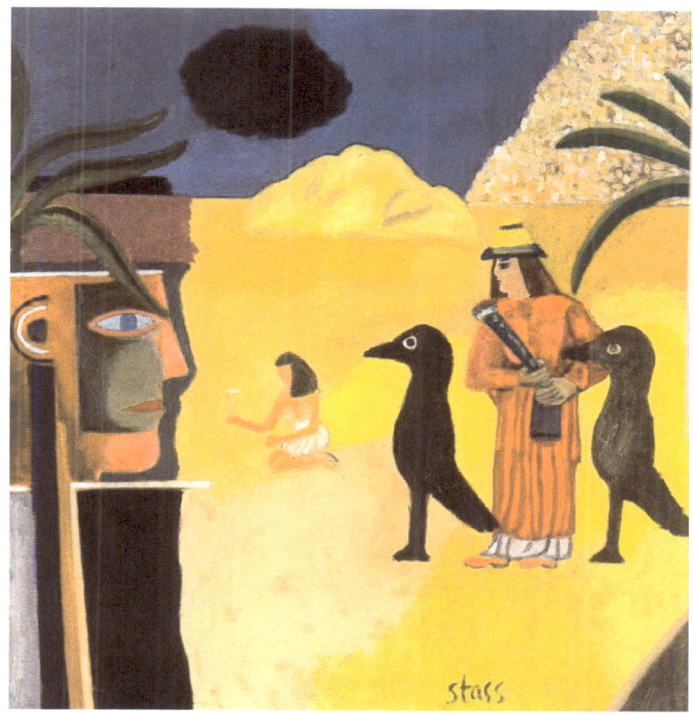

Memory of Egypt, oil on canvas, 1990

shelves with mirrors or home-made icons that used to be found in every Cypriot home (Greek, Turkish, Armenian or Maronite). Paraskos's constructions were crudely and brightly painted and decorated with images of film stars, cut from old copies of *The Picture Post.* Again it was the spirit of Cypriotness – innocent, brassy, open-hearted – that he was trying to convey. Yet he learnt too that he was flirting with the unacceptable. A restauranteur who commissioned some of the *objets d'art,* asking Paraskos to make him 'something Cypriot for his restaurant', decided against them when he saw them, and so these too now reside in Paraskos's own home.

Perhaps it is Paraskos's very cosmopolitanism that enables him to see the value in Cyprus's indigenous popular art whilst others hanker for Cypriots to adopt a

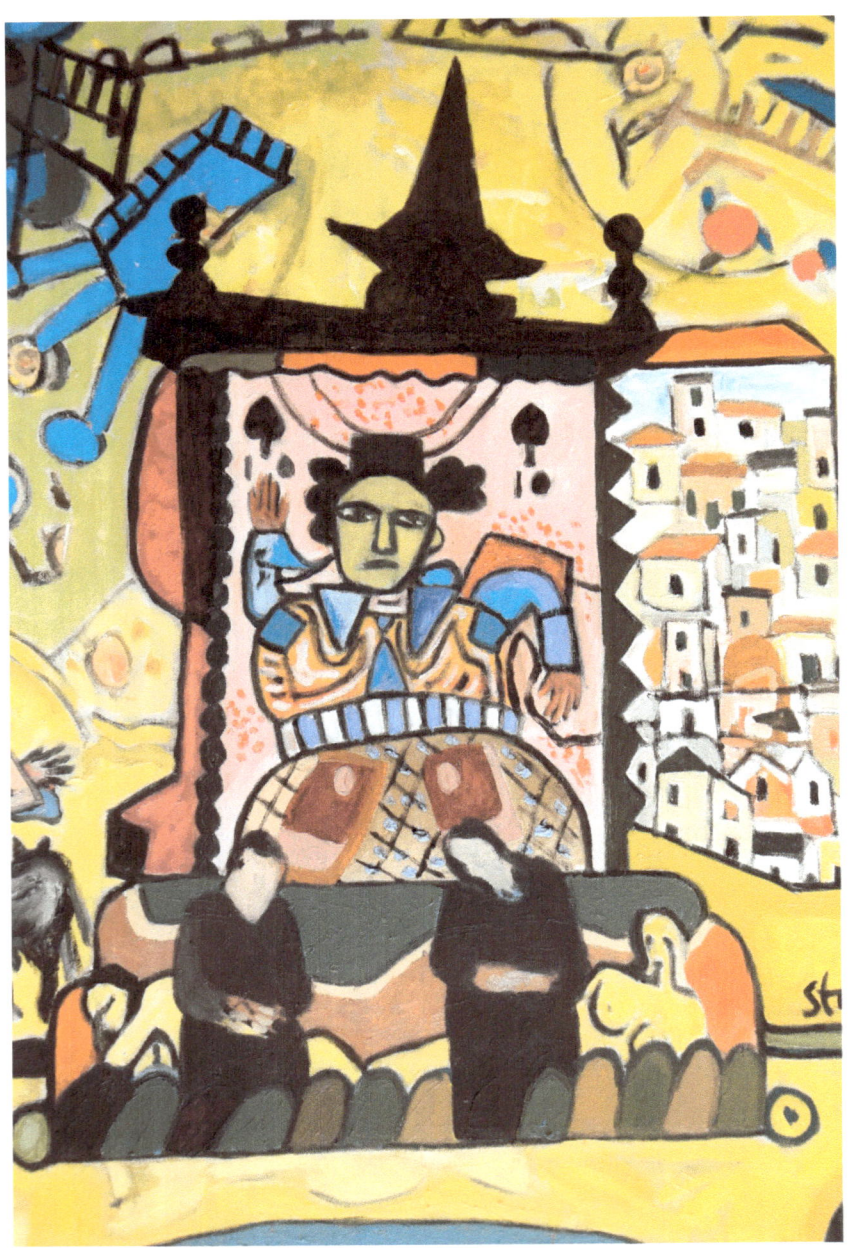

The Artist's Fantasy (The Dream), oil on canvas, 2008

European-style sophistication. Other finds have been old photographs from the twenties and thirties. In one a family stands beside an olive tree on a dusty road to a village. The mother stands with her hand on the shoulder of the youngest boy. There is a goat. An old man in his Sunday best stands proudly by his bicycle. The poses are rather stiff and formal, but the faces are calm and trusting. The whole design is hieratic, iconic again, and Paraskos likes these images enough to use them in his own art. To him they exude the simple spirit of an almost disappeared world, a pre-modern world of connecting bonds and strong feeling.

Not all of Paraskos's art is this kind of 'pop art'. He also makes human-sized constructed figures that are brightly and decoratively painted. They suggest Picasso, whom Paraskos admires greatly, but they also call to mind the eastern Mediterranean decorative art of the Bronze Age – such as one might see in the Cyprus Museum in Nicosia. These are, of course, the very kind of artefacts that inspired Picasso in the first instance, and their influence is nowhere more apparent than in the giant sculpture wall that Paraskos has constructed around the Cyprus College of Art's campus in the village of Lempa, itself a Bronze Age settlement. Paraskos is well-schooled in Chagall too, as well as other European art of a similar ilk, but he has travelled in Syria and Egypt and speaks admiringly of the historic and traditional arts of these countries. Together with the work itself, this suggest Paraskos draws inspiration as much from the relief statuary of Assyria and Egyptian wall painting, as from the Cypriot-Byzantine tradition and from Western art.

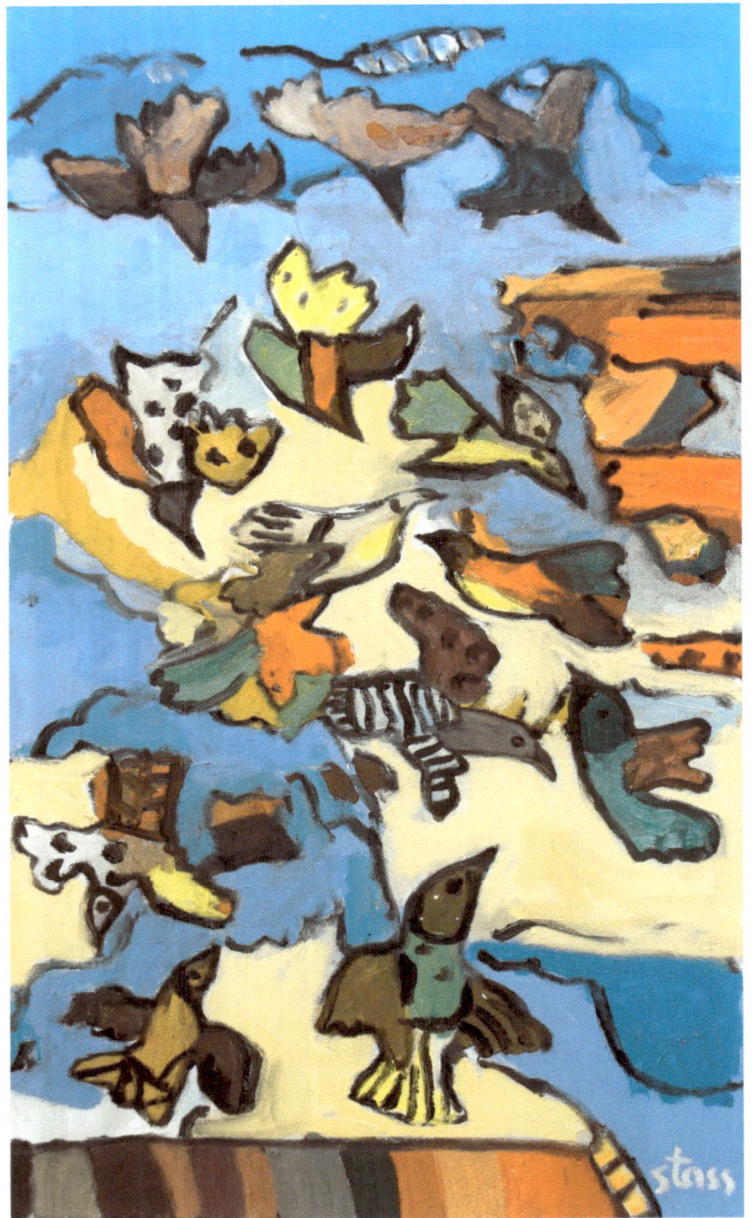

The Birds of Cyprus, oil on canvas, 2008

STASS'S COLLEGE OF ART

Michael Paraskos

The Cyprus College of Art is Stass and Stass is the Cyprus College of Art. As distinct entities the two are inseparable, and rather like the great art schools and studio-workshops of the past, this symbiotic relationship between the artist and the place the artist teaches gives to the Cyprus College of Art a unique and very special personality. It is the personality of Stass.

It is almost too easy at this point to roll out a criticism of some of the university art departments that have come to dominate art education in the rest of the world. Certainly it is true to say that studying art at Stass Paraskos's Cyprus College of Art is a very different experience of art education to that at, say, a university art school in London. Whilst Stass's students are in a unique and highly individual environment where the personality of a particular artist with a particular point of view has an impact on their work, those studying in a corporate university face the prospect of a corporate approach to art, which is rather like trying to learn *cordon bleu* cookery by working at MacDonalds. At one time all art schools in Britain, Europe and more or less everywhere else in the world were more like Stass's art school than a university, and they each had a particular personality and point of view. Now, however, Stass's place is one of a very small group of rare, but extremely precious, institutions that maintain their roots in a time when the art world aspired to greatness.

Stass would, I think, be happy with this aspiration, and certainly in his writings he has lamented the lack of ambition of too many artists working today. As he wrote in the early publicity for the College, the aim of the Cyprus College of Art is to provide a working space for people who see themselves as 'the artists of the future', and he has been particularly critical of those artists who turn art into a plaything or intellectual game. Art might have subject matter, and might seek to convey meaning, but it is never an illustration of clever mental concepts,

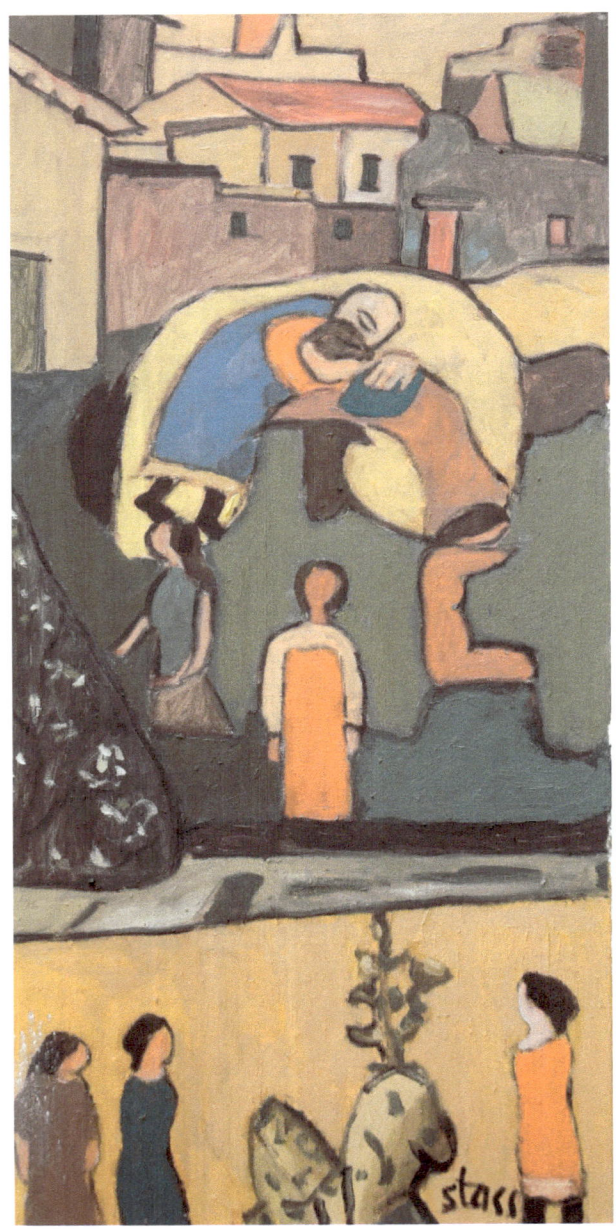

Embrace, oil on canvas, 2008

or a mere reflection of the world as it is. Like the Byzantine artists whose work filled the church in Stass's home village of Anaphotia, near Larnaca, and which he says was almost the only art he saw before he went to England, painting is a window into another reality, another world, and not a simple reflection of ordinary reality, or the ordinary world. Stass tells his students that art is always rooted in a direct experience, and specifically a direct visual experience, of being alive in this world, but that does not mean the artist can simply present aspects of this world to an audience and call it art. For art to exist a transformation – one might suggest, again in religious terms, a transubstantiation – has to take place to turn the ordinary reality of life into the extraordinary hyper-reality of art.

Of course this might, in itself, suggest that Stass's teaching is vague and theoretical, but nothing could be further from the truth. Like all the best artists who are the best teachers, his advice to students is often simple, straightforward and practical. As a lover of colour in his own art, he is particularly fond of teaching his students colour theory, whilst in tutorials students might be advised to make their forms and colours stronger, or to improve the sense of balance in a composition by adding an element in a particular place on the canvas, or to disrupt a composition to create a sense of surprise by adding an unexpected element, and so on. When this works the praise is not usually couched in critical language – as few real artists ever talk in such terms – but is more likely to be phrased as 'good', 'great' or, when he is really enthused, as 'fantastic'.

The Cyprus College of Art itself was started by Stass in 1969, when he was working as a tutor at Leeds College of Art. There are a few newspaper articles from Cyprus that show Stass had been thinking of the idea for at least a couple of years before this, and he must have raised it with officials in Cyprus, but still there is a sense

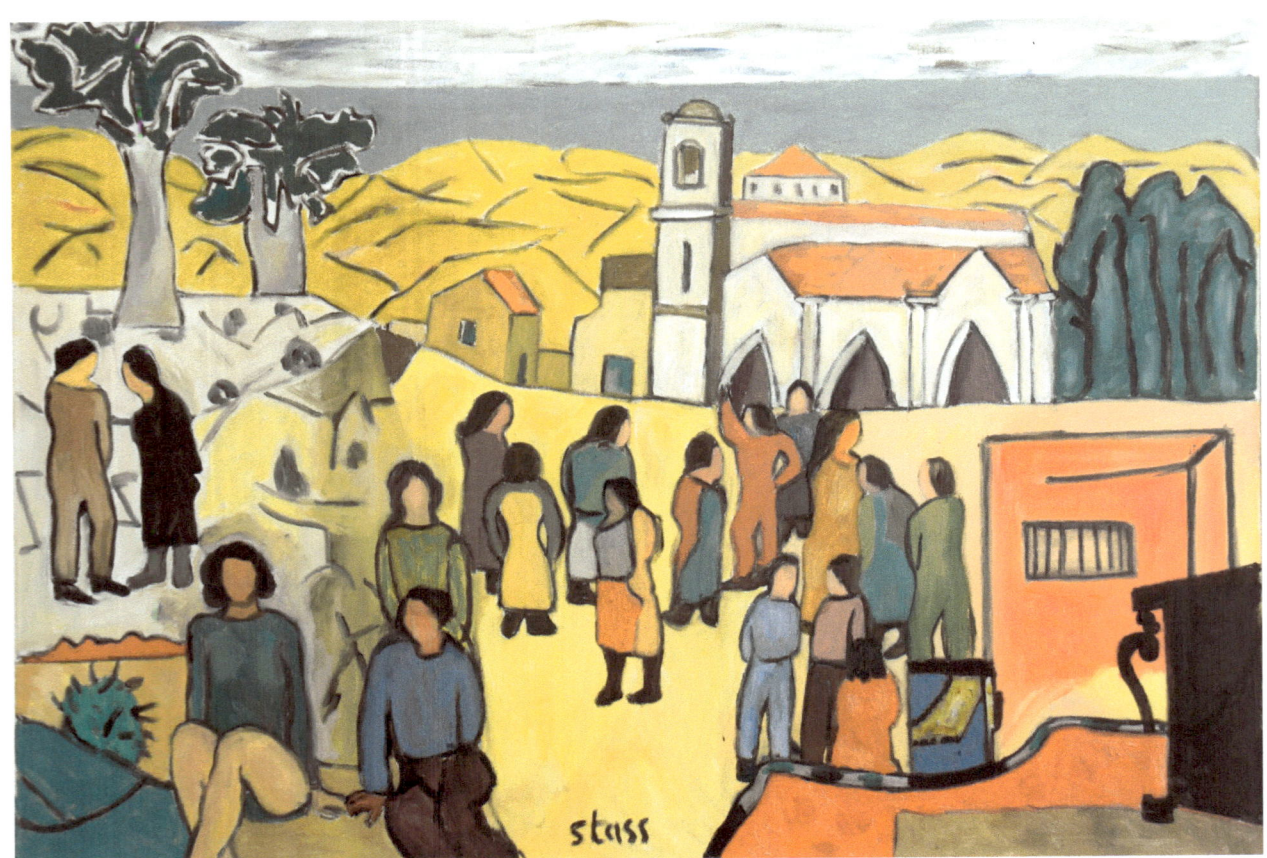

Sunday Afternoon, oil on canvas, 2008

that the real origin of the Cyprus College of Art lies in some half-serious discussion over a pint or two of beer at one of the pubs frequented by the artists and art students of Leeds – perhaps the Coburg, or Fenton, or Eldon. Whatever the truth, by the summer of 1969, in the aftermath of the year of revolutions, a group of artists, art students, poets and assorted hangers-on led by Stass set out *en-masse,* from Leeds to London to catch a plane to Cyprus

It is difficult to capture the bravery of this act now as we are used to hassle-free travel across Europe, low-cost airlines, and many British students show no qualms about spending their summers in South East Asia, South America and increasingly Africa. In 1969, however, package tourism even to Spain was only just beginning, and almost no tourists went to Cyprus, where a vicious war against British colonial rule had ended less than a decade earlier, and a low-level civil war was sill apparent. As well as brave, the journey was uncertain and the group from Leeds arrived in London only to find there was no plane waiting for them. Inexplicably, it had been cancelled. Their travel agent gave them a choice. They could either have a refund, or he would book them on the train to Athens, from where they could catch the ferry to Cyprus. With the exception of Eric Taylor, the Principal of Leeds College of Art, and his wife, everyone opted to take the train to Athens.

As Stass tells it, the journey was an adventure, most notably in Greece where the military dictatorship that ruled the country had recently banned boys from having long hair and girls from wearing miniskirts. When the group of long haired hippy boys and trendy art school girls in miniskirts from Leeds turned up in Athens they were almost arrested on the spot. As a Greek Stass was singled out for questioning and was accused of being a Communist (not far wrong as it turned out, but being a Communist was not something to admit to an

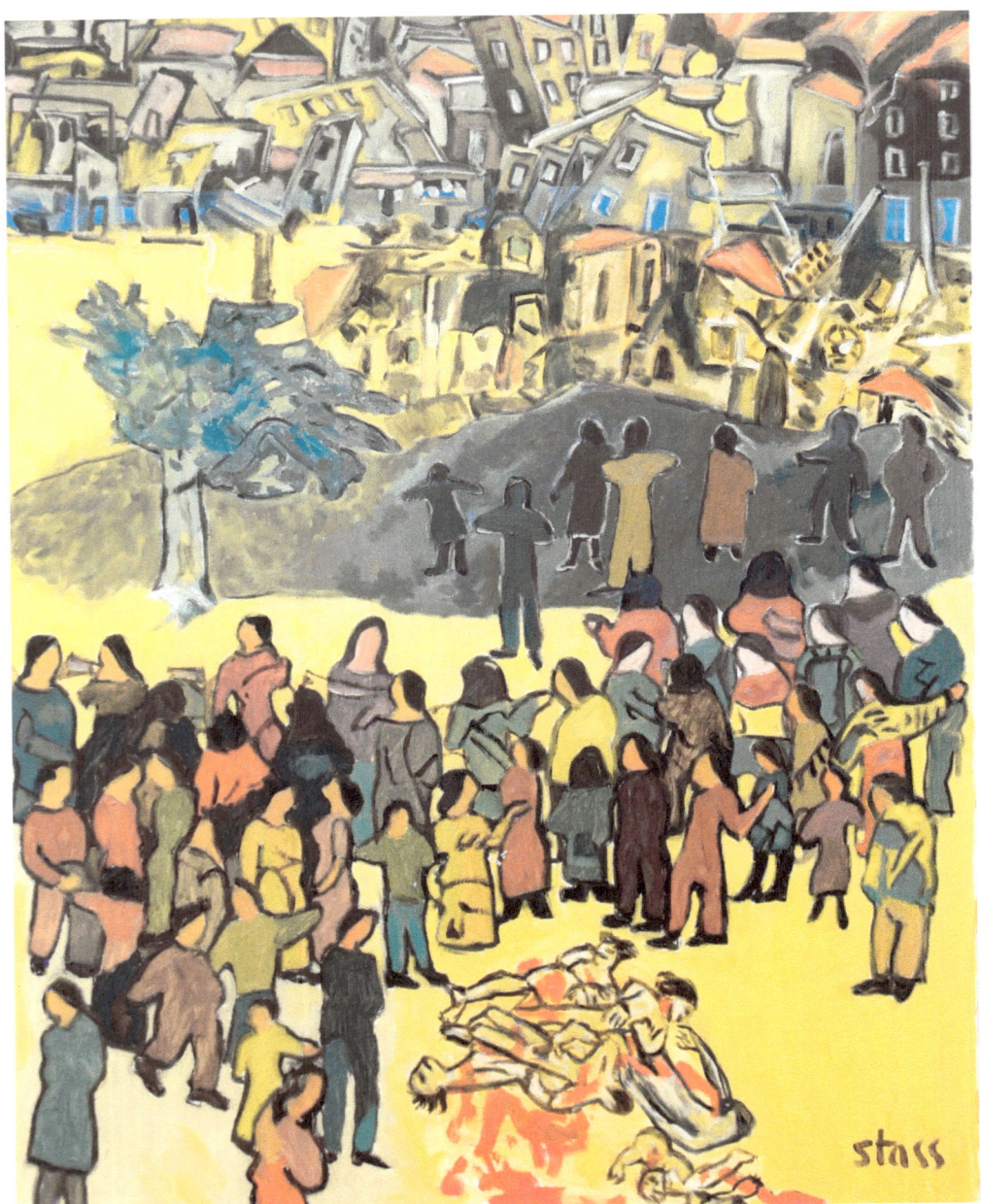

Massacre at Qana, oil on canvas, 2007

agent of a fascist junta). Thankfully, he managed to persuade the grim-faced immigration officer that they were not out to corrupt the Youth of Greece, but were simply *en-route* to Cyprus for a 'painting holiday'. Like all fascists, he was suspicious, but let them go.

The first Cyprus Summer School, as it was called, was important in setting the template for the Cyprus College of Art, with artists, students and poets mixing a serious commitment to making art with a strong sense of pleasure in the sun. In the spirit of the time, it was all about revolutionary freedom, but also about community and enjoying the company of other artists. To this day the Cyprus Summer School (now called the Cyprus Summer Studio) is run annually on the same basis, but there is also something of the Summer School even in the more formal courses run by the College. In a sense, the political passion for freedom that fired up revolutionary art tutors like Harry Thubron, and the students who took over Hornsey School of Art in 1968 - and where Stass had in fact taught - was present in those first Cyprus Summer Schools, but that political passion was humanised, partly by the warmth of the Mediterranean sunshine, but mainly by the personality of Stass himself.

For the next few of years the Summer School was repeated, each time being held in Famagusta, the main town on the east coast of Cyprus. Inevitably in 1969, Stass and the students had arrived in Cyprus with no money, having spent what little they had on their journey across Europe. Nor did they have any accommodation, but the trip was saved when Stass's friend, the Cypriot painter George Skotinos persuaded the local council in Famagusta to lend Stass a school to use as dormitory accommodation for the artists during the summer.

Despite this, it didn't take long for the businessmen of Famagusta to realise that 'Stass's tourists', as they called the students, never had any

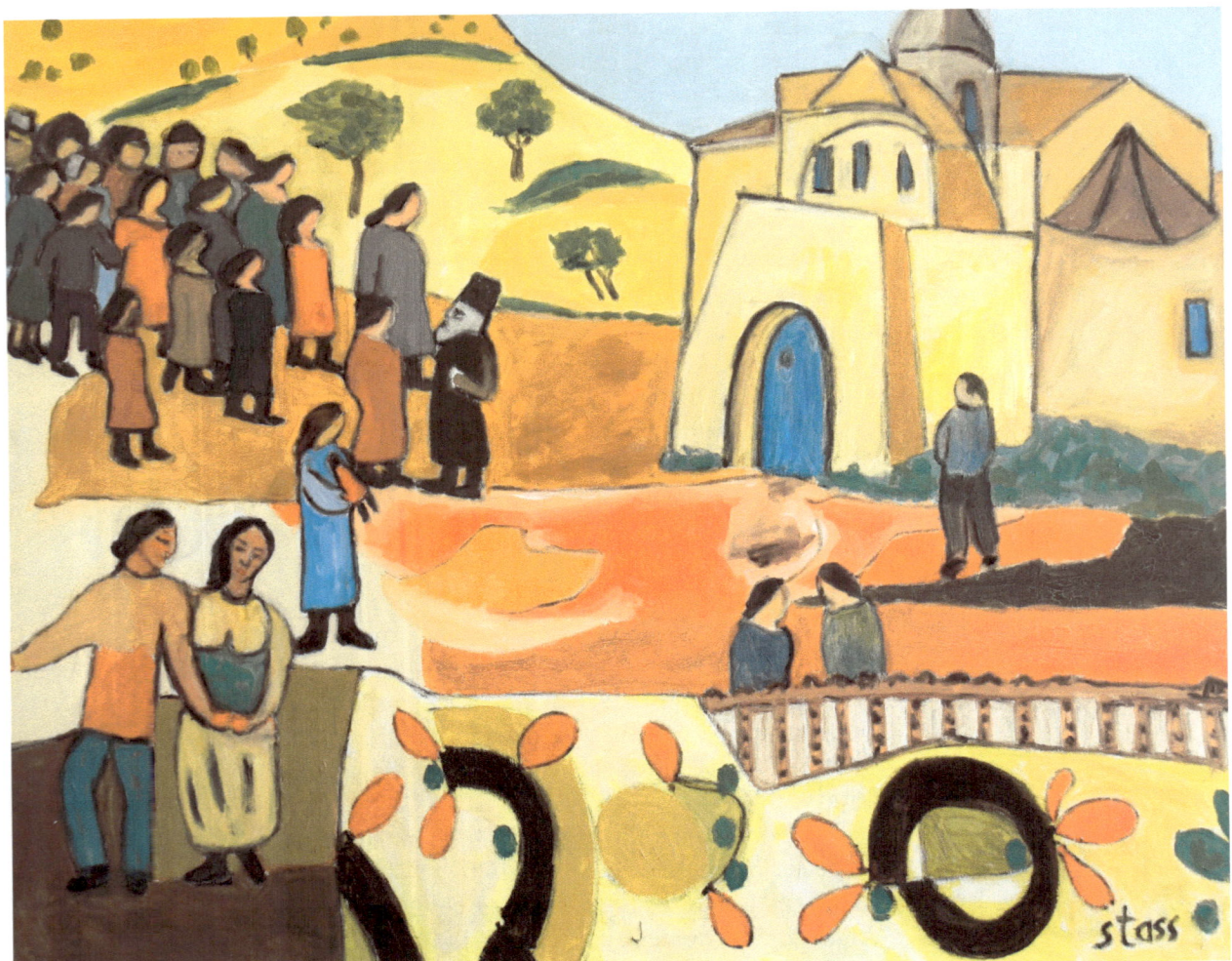

Going to Church, oil on canvas, 2008

money, even when they managed to fly to Cyprus directly. And, as mass-tourism began to take over the town, Famagusta decided it didn't want any more penniless artists painting in its streets. It was then that another Cypriot artist, Costas Economou, came to the rescue by persuading the town council in Paphos, on the once-unfashionable west coast of the island, to house Stass's Summer School. With this move, in 1973, the idea of creating a permanent and year-round college of art for Cyprus seems to have taken a real hold, and Stass would have probably created the Cyprus College of Art in 1974 or 1975 had the Turkish army not invaded Cyprus in the summer of 1974, throwing everything into chaos. Despite Cyprus losing almost half its territory to the invaders, and facing a major refugee crisis, the astonishing fact is that Stass was able to restart the Summer School in 1976, and in 1978 to turn it into the Cyprus College of Art by launching a year-round course, called the Postgraduate Diploma in Fine Art. As with the Summer School, this too still exists today, and attracts students mainly from Britain, Ireland, Europe and North America, and sometimes even as far away as Australia.

In many ways these early years of the College, coinciding with the early years of Cyprus as an independent country, represent a more innocent time both for the College and Cyprus. One suspects Stass was more at home in the Cyprus that existed then than he is in the Cyprus that started to develop in the 1980s and which dominates today. Stass still knows the political leaders of Cyprus well, but the days when he could take a group of art students from Leeds to have tea, almost on the spur of the moment, with the President of Cyprus – and the celebrated President Archbishop Makarios at that! – have long gone. Yet it happened back then when Stass, the English poet Martin Bell and the students were given coffee and ice cream by the President. Similarly there is a touching innocence in the story Stass tells of the first year of the postgraduate course when the students, most of whom came from Britain, were suddenly desperate to see snow. Hearing of snowfall on Mount Troodos they insisted Stass hire a bus to take them into the mountains to see it. Unfortunately the journey on the old mountain roads took so long that all the snow had melted by the time they got there.

Perhaps it was that innocence that also led to an astonishing level of generosity towards Stass and his art school from other artists in the art world, which meant he was able to attract so many big names in British art to teach at the College. Often they took no pay, sometimes even paying their own fares, and amongst their names are some great artists, including Terry Frost, Mali Morris, Michael Kidner, Jon Isherwood, Dennis Creffield, Jennifer Durrant, Euan Uglow, Peter de Francia, Geoff Rigden and many others. They came to the College in Cyprus for a simple love of art and the friendship of Stass, and not for financial reward.

Like Stass, the Cyprus College of Art is still going strong as an institution, and now has new accredited courses and premises. It has formal links with foreign universities, and more students study at it than ever before. Stass still teaches at the College and the ethos of the place remains rooted in the experiences of those early years. It remains an art school dreamt up in a pub in Leeds. Nonetheless, it is difficult not to look on the 1970s and 80s as some kind of golden age for the College. That is not meant to sound a sombre note, it is simply to recognise that there is always something more exciting and endearing about institutions run by warm-hearted people, who are able to fly by the seat of their pants in tolerant environments, working on a shoestring, rather than those that have bureaucracies to support them. It is strange but true, in art too much technology and too many facilities actually hinders creativity. But Cyprus has also changed and today if we even want to put up a garden shed in the College yard we have to gain planning permission in writing beforehand; in 1985 Stass and the Summer School tutors and students built an entire 'suite' of studios without even thinking to ask anyone.

All of which means that when we look at Stass's Cyprus College of Art to-day we can see clearly that it has two aspects. The first is shown by the College's campus in Lempa, a small village near Paphos. There we can see an institution that still resembles the College of the '70s and '80s, with all the improvisation and freedom that implies, but also with leaky roofs and dodgy plumbing. The second is in Larnaca, where there is a very nice building that probably most closely resembles a standard college of art, even down to having an office, library and computers. No one can deny it is nice to have the relative comfort and ease of the Larnaca site, but I think anyone with an artistic soul would always long for the spirit of Lempa, even with its slightly ramshackle appearance and primitive conditions. It is unique, and proof positive that the Cyprus College of Art is Stass's most important work of Art.

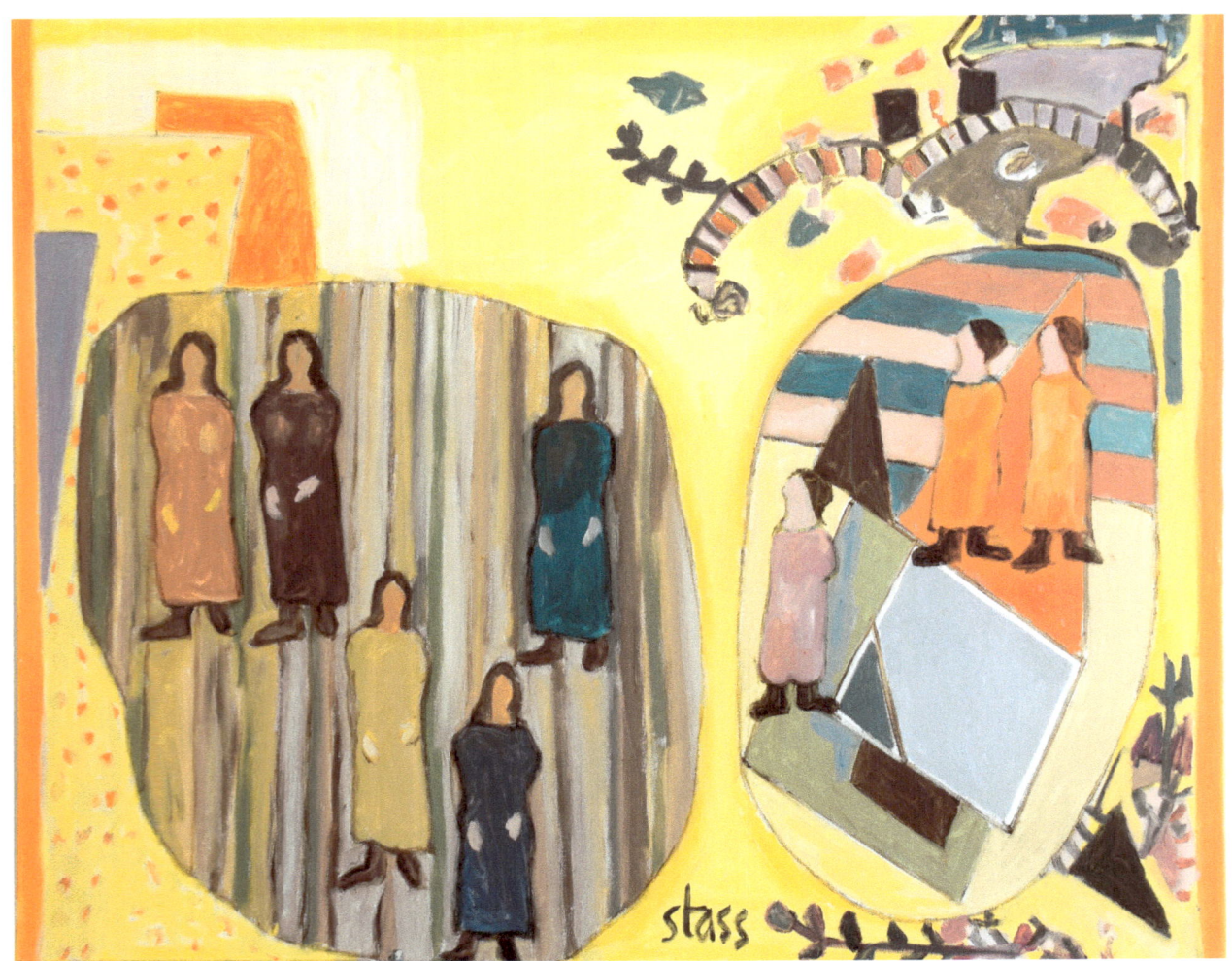

Figure Composition, oil on canvas, 2007

STASS AT CANTERBURY

David Haste

Stass taught at Canterbury College of Art, first as a visiting part-timer, then eighteen years as a full time lecturer. Unlike the rest of us, he held no degree, diploma or formal qualifications but possessed other inestimable teaching credentials. While working at his brother's restaurant in the 1950s, he had first enrolled as a part-time student at Leeds College of Art. There, he came under the spell of an art education genius, Harry Thubron and participated in Thubron's transformation of Leeds into a leading national art school. After a year in the painters' colony at St Ives, Stass took up his first teaching job with another formidable art teacher, Tom Hudson at Leicester. Although his overriding ambition was to be a professional artist, Stass discovered a second vocation in art teaching and carried with him these early formative examples into his own subsequent role as a teacher.

Tom Watt, then Head of Fine Art at Canterbury, who had known Stass at Leeds, made him a full time painting lecturer in 1971, the same year the art college moved to a new campus in the city. These were heady times for art schools - what some refer to as 'the golden age', with small numbers of students, abundant resources and part time teaching, a constant flow of visiting artists and relative freedom to develop ambitious art courses within the new diploma [DipAD] culture. Stass became part of Watt's 'metaphysical school', which, whilst managing to be orthodox and laissez-faire at the same time, expected the teacher and the taught to share an untrammelled passion for colour, strong intuition, dedicated studios and unfettered 'expression', out of which art might 'generate itself'. Or as Humphrey Ocean, one of Stass's earlier painting students, described it, 'learning by osmosis'. The subjective pace of teaching suited Stass's temperament but this alone proved insufficient to meet his increasing appetite for ideas, criticism and self-taught authorship. Amongst the many

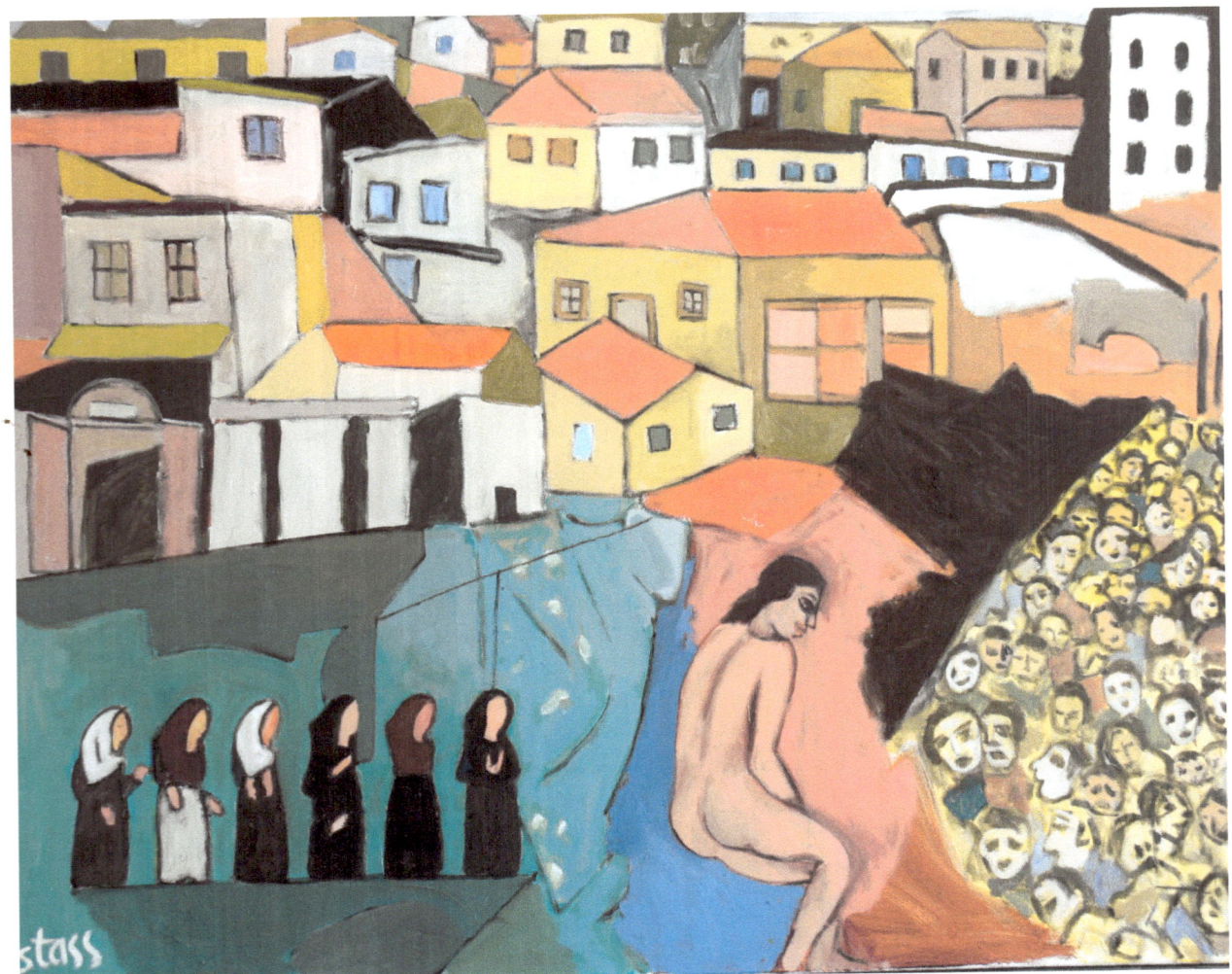

Red Nude, oil on canvas, 2007

part timers and visitors, Stass cultivated a wide ranging familiarity with contemporary art and above all the company of other artists. The seventies art colleges saw the rise of theoretical studies whose increased relevance was meant to put the shine on the new 'degree status' and compliment practice-based studio subjects, but for Tom Watt, and others like him, such newcomers were seen as alien, incursive, politicised and even subversive. Stass liked Toni del Renzio, the head of art history, and became increasingly concerned as the fracture between theory and practice, then rife throughout art education, developed into an ever deepening schism across the college dividing loyalties amongst students as well as staff. This state of affairs culminated in what Stass has described as the 'CNAA tragedy' when the National Council threatened to withdraw approval, which in turn would have closed down Fine Art at Canterbury.

I became Head of Fine Art at the beginning of 1982 as the pieces were being put together again and, in the restructuring that followed, Stass's support in resetting the school's compass proved invaluable and our friendship developed from there. Our first collaboration was an exhibition of Vanessa Bell's paintings at the Royal Museum where I came to recognise his great love of painting and the generosity he extended towards a diversity of styles. Stass has always believed in the integrity of making art and a full engagement with whatever activity was involved. He would often work alongside students in one of the painting studios or the bronze foundry or etching room. I can't remember Stass ever being doctrinaire, his teaching was individual, seemingly relaxed but quite incisive. At Canterbury he characteristically held back during group crits, observing while curling some piece of wood or wire picked up from the studio floor between his fingers, then, when so much had been said, he would open up and deliver his own judgement. Interrogation of students' work was

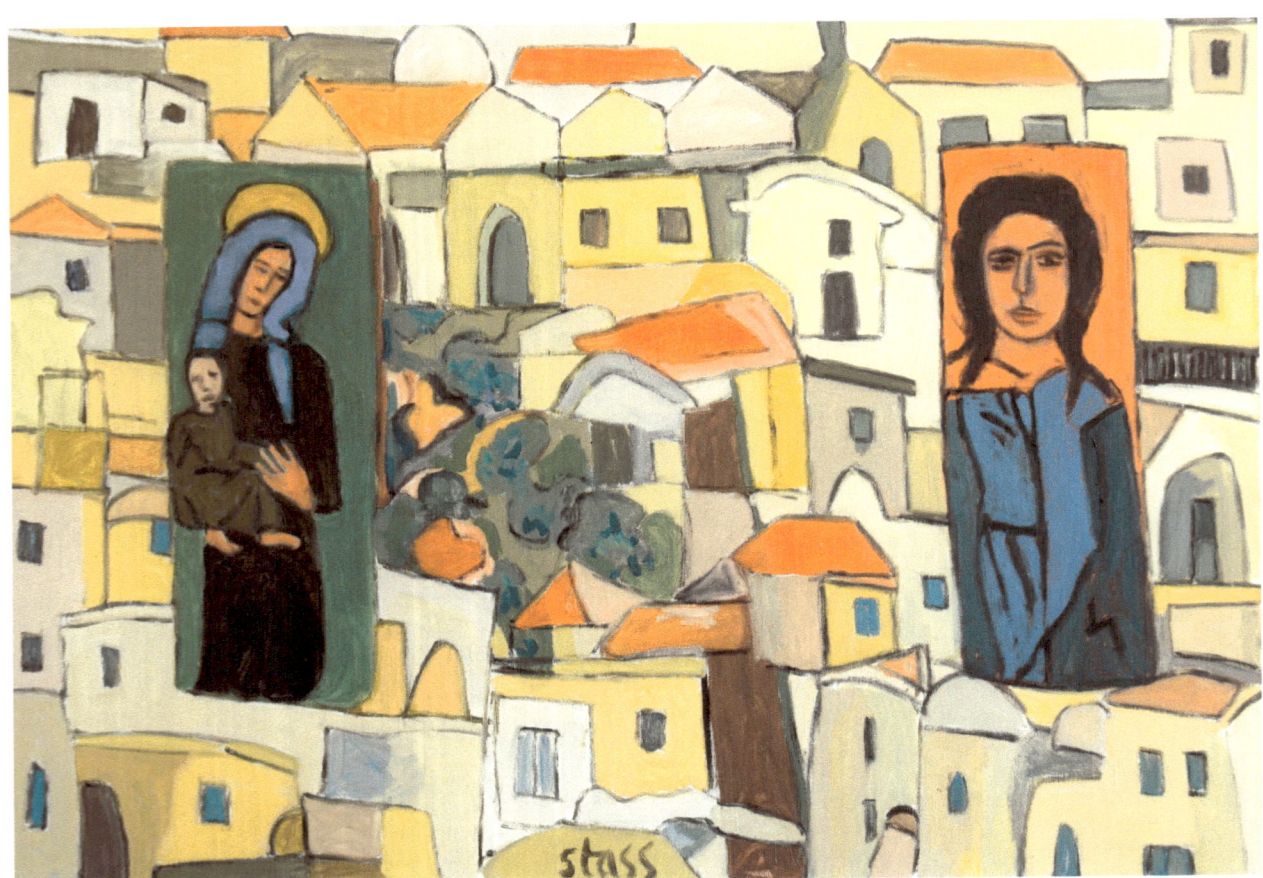

Saints of the Village, oil on canvas, 2007

authoritative but rarely forced and his commentaries and criticisms, above all, were always delivered with warmth and support. Stass's temperament perfectly matched the ambience of the Canterbury painting studios, which Adrian Heath recognised during one of his visits as, 'a feeling of happiness and contentment... a hedonistic pleasure in light and colour, where a lurking sense of magic was very real.'

I recall a meeting of tutors from both studio and art history at which we were rehearsing our responses for some imminent inquisition. Evidence of theory seemed somewhat thin on the ground so I asked around the table if anyone had ever written a book that had been published. Only one hand was raised, it was Stass, who modestly revealed himself as an author and one translated into several languages. As a teacher, Stass hated academic snobbery but always respected knowledge from whatever source and actively encouraged students to read as well as look. He was, by and large, self taught but always avowed a very deep respect for learning. In 1985 the college built the first 'A1 listed' art gallery at any Kent college and the Academic Board's indecision about naming it was only resolved once Stass suggested it be called the Herbert Read Gallery after one of this country's most eminent art critics and erstwhile defender of Stass's paintings against alleged pornography at an exhibition in 1966.

By the mid 1980s, change was sweeping through art education and Kent was about to receive the brunt of so called 'rationalisation', or as Patrick Heron wrote of it after a visit to a besieged Canterbury in 1986, 'art schools being torn to shreds and fine art courses plunged into the darkest Victorian night'. Treating students as potential artists was to be 'diverted' towards other goals, fine art courses came under ominous threats and the authorities deemed that Kent's three remaining Kent art colleges were too small and inadequate to match the new template of art education. It was to be merger or nothing. In 1987 the Kent art colleges combined and another reality emerged, the Kent Institute of Art and Design. Now, after another recent merger with Surrey, this has dissolved into the University for the Creative Arts. The disruption to what had once been a small familial fine art school at Canterbury was immense. Everything would change. The old course for existing students was permitted to remain until they graduated and Stass became their subject leader in painting for the remaining two years while a wholly new course was constructed alongside to comply with the new order. The ethos of the 'atelier' was fading fast and Stass, feeling more like a lost species, was looking for a way out. He retired from Canterbury in 1989. After all, he had his own art school in Cyprus, the Cyprus College of Art at Lemba where the older values he so cherished could still prevail and where he would continue to teach.

Several years later when Stass and I escaped the Cypriot heat under the shade of a tree at Kissonerga he reminisced about his art teaching years in England. Although reflecting on those last seven years at Canterbury as good years, he resented the changes following the mergers and the phenomenal growth of the Kent Institute that left him feeling increasingly an outsider. He remains an 'art school' animal in the old sense, a belief in the organic nature of artistic development and teaching in a studio, preferably one to one beside the student's easel. He liked art schools when they were small units with a character of their own, not the burgeoning institutions and quasi-universities that have rapidly replaced them. Yet he confessed that, however much he enjoyed his last years in Kent, he just couldn't feel sentimental about Canterbury any more, for him Leeds remained 'his art school' and that was where his heart would always belong.

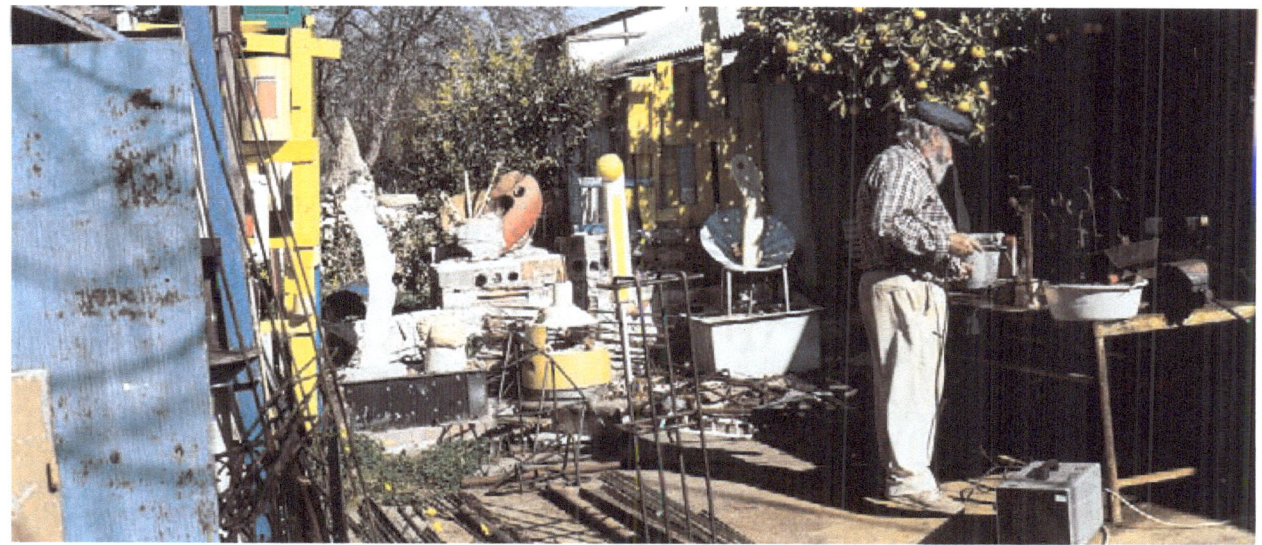

Stass at Work on the Sculpture Wall at the Cyprus College of Art, Lempa (Paphos), 2006

ISBN 978-0-9544523-5-3

Published by The **Orage** Press

Special thanks go to Terry Jones, Mary Paraskos,
Andreas Efstathiou and the contributors to this volume.

We would also like to thank Leeds College of Art and Design and
the Cyprus College of Art.

The **Orage** Press
16a Heaton Road, Mitcham, Surrey CR4 2BU, England.

www.ingramcontent.com/pod-product-compliance
Lightning Source LLC
Chambersburg PA
CBHW050833110526
45159CB00004B/1884